"Let food be thy medicine"
~Hippocrates

www.ClassicalLearner.com

Little Bears it's time to read,
About the birds and trees and seeds.
Dirt and water and the sun,
Make peanuts grow and rabbits run.
Look outside, that plant that grew,
In a lot of ways, it's part of you.

Carrots, apples, plums, and peas,
All start out as little seeds.

Plant that seed right in the ground,
Sprouts shoot up and roots grow down.
They grow, they twist, they reach, they coil,
Magic happens in the soil.

Bugs and sand and dust are small,
But to bacteria they aren't small at all.
Bacteria, viruses, and fungi too,

Are part of the dirt and part of you.
These tiny things are hard to see,
We call them microbiology.

When dead bugs and leaves fall to the ground,
Bacteria and fungi gather around.
Bears and lions and tigers and crows,
Bacteria make them decompose.
Leaves and paws and tails and feet,
Bacteria are what bacteria eat.

When dead plants and animals are broken down,
Nutrients are released into the ground.
Vitamin A,B,C, and K,
Are all released when animals decay.
Potassium, magnesium, sulfur, and calcium too,
These minerals are good for plants and good for you.

Vitamin (A)

Healthy soil, water, and sun,
Allow plants to grow and cats to
run.
Vitamins and minerals are
absorbed by plant roots,
They use the ingredients to make
vegetables and fruits.
Do you like the taste of this? And
this?
It's made possible by
photosynthesis.

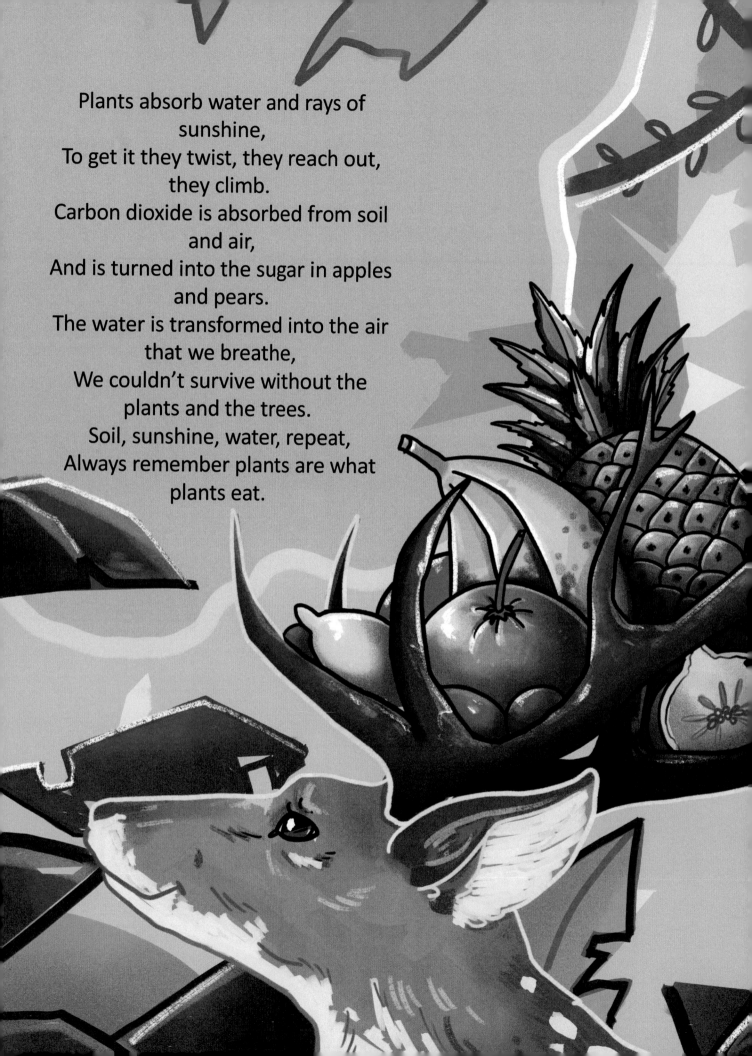

Plants absorb water and rays of
sunshine,
To get it they twist, they reach out,
they climb.
Carbon dioxide is absorbed from soil
and air,
And is turned into the sugar in apples
and pears.
The water is transformed into the air
that we breathe,
We couldn't survive without the
plants and the trees.
Soil, sunshine, water, repeat,
Always remember plants are what
plants eat.

Bananas and grass and leaves and mushrooms,
Are delicious foods that animals consume.
Nutrients, vitamins, and minerals too
Are digested by monkeys and caribou.
Grass, fruits, vegetables, chicken legs, and cow meat.
Animals are what animals eat.

Eating healthy makes you grow big and
strong,
It's how ears grow big, and giraffe necks
grow long.
Berries, bananas, cows, fish, and pears,
Will help you to grow as strong as a
Bear.
Nutrients and vitamins and minerals
too,
They transfer from plants and animals
to you.
From your hands to your arms to your
legs and your feet,
Always remember you are what you
eat.

Write an Amazon review ! ! !

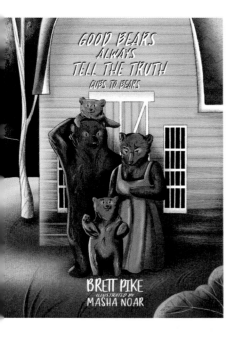

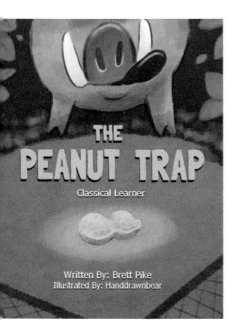

Use discount code "cubstobears" for $5.00's off Classical Learner's "Homeschools Connected."

Made in the USA
Las Vegas, NV
30 September 2023

78334908R00017